Working with

CHILDREN

Diane Church

W
FRANKLIN WATTS
LONDON·SYDNEY

Many of the photographs in this book
feature real people in difficult circumstances.
Because of this, some of the photographs may not
be as clear or bright as we would normally wish.

This edition 2004

Franklin Watts
96 Leonard Street
London EC2A 4XD

Franklin Watts Australia
45-51 Huntley Street
Alexandria
NSW 2015

© 2001 Franklin Watts

Editor: Kate Banham
Art Direction: Jason Anscomb

Acknowledgements
The publishers would like to thank the following people and organisations
for their permission to reproduce photographs in this book:
ActionAid: 23 (both); Action Research: 4, 5 (bottom), 8; Anti-Slavery International: 22;
John Birdsall: 8; ChildLine: Larry Bray 7, 18, 19 (top); Children's Country Holidays Fund: 15 (bottom);
The Children's Society: front cover, 13, 14 (bottom), 15 (top); Format: Sharon Baseley 5 (top), Paula Glassman 14 (top);
Franklin Watts: 6, 19 (bottom); Jubilee Action: Matt Roper 21 (both); Bob Kauders: 11, 17; Kirsteen Lupton: 10;
NCH Action for Children: 16, 26 (both); NSPCC: Tony Sapiano 27; The Refugee Council: Maggie Lambert 24;
Save the Children: David Stewart-Smith 25 (both); Scope: 12; Third Avenue Ltd: Jon Walter 20;
UNICEF: 9 (top: HQ95-0979/Shehzad Noorani), (bottom: HQ94-0240/Betty Press).

A CIP catalogue record for this book is available from the British Library

ISBN: 0 7496 5612 3

Printed in Malaysia

Contents

What is a charity? 4

Problems at school 6

Finding a cure 8

Being ill 10

Joining in 12

No money 14

A loving family 16

Safe from harm 18

No home 20

Around the world 22

War time 24

Raising money 26

How you can help 28

Glossary 29

Contact addresses 30

Index 32

Words printed in **bold** are explained in the glossary.

♥ What is a charity?

We all need help sometimes. Maybe you've been ill and stayed in hospital. Or you've been frightened and your mum or dad or a teacher helped you.

Some people need lots of help because they don't have the special things we all need to be happy. Here are some of the things we need:

- health
- proper food
- somewhere safe to live
- someone to love

What else do you think all children need to be happy?

Charities help people who do not have these things. This book shows how some charities help children.

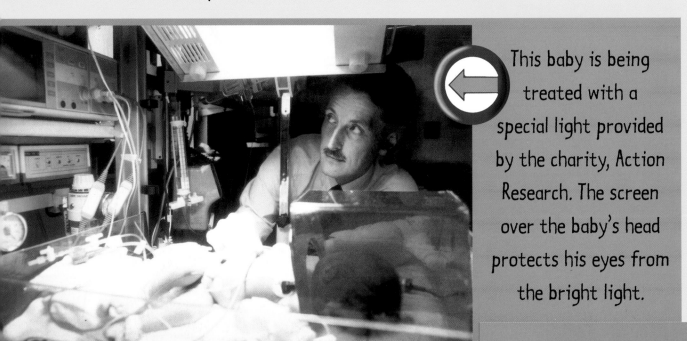

This baby is being treated with a special light provided by the charity, Action Research. The screen over the baby's head protects his eyes from the bright light.

Some families would not have enough money to buy children all they need without help from charities.

Charities help people who live in very poor areas. Together they improve housing, play areas and safety.

Famous people, children and businesses all help raise money for charities.

Problems at school

Everyone has problems at school. At times, you may have fallen out with your friends, got into trouble or found it hard to understand your school work.

Charities help children, teachers, mums and dads find ways to sort out these problems so that school is a happy, interesting place to be.

You need to be happy if you are going to do well at school.

CASE STUDY

Rachel used to be picked on by other children in the playground. She was so unhappy she didn't want to go to school. Then she made a free phone call to ChildLine, a charity helpline for children who have a problem (see page 30). The woman on the phone helped Rachel see that she needed to talk to her mum or dad so they could help stop the bullying.

What would you do if you had a problem at school?

Each year lots of children become very ill because they catch an illness that has no cure.

Some charities develop new medicines to make these children better again. They also try to find new medicines to stop people becoming ill in the first place.

Some diseases can make you very weak. You may need sticks to help you walk, or you may have to use a wheelchair.

In the 1950s doctors – helped by the charity Action Research – developed a new medicine to prevent an illness called **polio**. At the time thousands of children were dying of polio each year. Many more were **disabled** by the illness, which meant they could not walk, move around or breathe without help.

Since doctors started giving the new medicine, children in Britain no longer become ill with polio.

Now, all around the world, children are being given the polio medicine when they are small. This is being organised by a group of charities led by UNICEF.

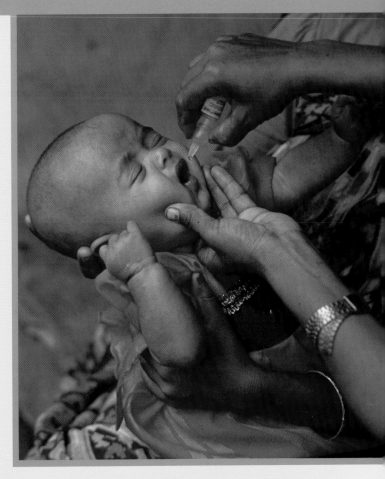

These children are being given medicine to prevent them catching measles.

Ask your mum or dad what medicine you've had to stop you becoming ill.

♡ Being ill

We all get ill sometimes. But there are children who are very sick and have to spend a lot of time in hospital. They miss being with their family and friends, going to school and having fun.

CASE STUDY

Kirsteen (7, shown here with her father and brothers) recently had to stay in hospital for over a month. The hospital, Great Ormond Street, was hundreds of miles from her home. The hospital's charity provided a room for her family to stay in, so Kirsteen wouldn't be alone.

What would you miss most if you had to go into hospital for a long time?

Talking to someone about something that has upset you helps you to understand your feelings.

Occasionally a mum or dad may become so ill that they die. How would you feel if something happened to your mum or dad? The charity Cruse Bereavement Care helps children talk about what's happened so they can feel a bit better.

Joining in

Do you have any friends who sometimes find it difficult to join in with what you're doing? Why is that? It may be because they cannot use a part of their body in the same way as you, or because they have to help out a lot at home.

CASE STUDY

Aimee (6) was born with a condition that makes it harder for her to move around, speak and see. But she wants to do the same things as other children her age. The charity Scope helped train Aimee's teachers and provided someone to help her in class. She can now read and write and go to her local school with her friends.

It is very important that
all children get a chance to laugh
and play with their friends.

If your mum or dad was sick, you would probably have to do more chores like washing and shopping. Some charities, such as Barnardo's, help children whose parents are ill a lot. They make sure these children do not miss out going to school and playing with their friends.

How could you look after your mum or dad if they couldn't get out of bed?

♥ No money

If you had to give up one of the following – your toys, your house, some of your meals or hot water – which would you choose?

Lots of children miss out on one or more of these things every day because their families do not have much money.

Some children live in homes where they have nowhere to play.

Charities like the Children's Society run family centres in poor areas with local mums and dads so children do not miss out on having fun – just because they have no spare money.

The Children's Society family centres have lots of interesting toys, activities and safe playgrounds.

Many families cannot afford to go on holiday. But they may get the chance to enjoy the countryside or seaside through the Children's Country Holidays Fund.

These children are enjoying a day out organised by the Children's Country Holidays Fund.

♥ A loving family

We all need someone special to care for us. That's what families are for.

But some mums and dads find it hard to look after their children. They may ignore them or be cruel.

What would you do if someone in your family hurt you?

Charities like NCH – Action for Children help mums and dads sort out their problems so that they can love their children better.

Sometimes it helps to talk about your problems with someone you don't know.

Sometimes charities have to find new families for children if things at home are very bad.

CASE STUDY

James (14) and Philip (13) were found a new family by the charity Barnardo's. Since being **adopted**, the boys are very happy with their new dad David, who says: 'We are a real family, just like any other normal, loving family.'

Has anyone ever said something horrible that made you cry? Or have you ever been hit or hurt in some way? If so, you probably felt very upset and frightened.

Some children feel like this all the time because they are picked on by other people. They may be forced to do things they don't want to or are hit and shouted at unfairly.

Children are not allowed to be **abused** in this way. Charities, like the National Society for the Prevention of Cruelty to Children (NSPCC), have a special phone number to ring if you know of anyone being hurt or are being hurt yourself (see page 31).

It is free to phone the NSPCC on their helpline.

After children have been frightened or harmed, they can sometimes feel better if they draw pictures to show what happened. The charity **Refuge** helps children in this way.

What would you do if you were treated badly or knew someone who was being hurt?

♥ No home

If you had no home to live in, where would you go? Maybe you could stay with your grandparents or some friends.

If you had no home of your own, you might have to sleep on a friend's sofa.

In Britain, charities like Centrepoint provide beds for **young people** who are **homeless**, and help them get a job so they have some money to pay for a place to live.

Around the world, the problem is much worse. There are millions of families who are too poor to have a home of their own.

CASE STUDY

Vivian (14) never knew her parents. She had to live on the streets in Brazil as she had no one to care for her. She now lives in a home run by Jubilee Action and goes to school. One day she wants to be a doctor.

Millions of children in Brazil have no home.

What would be the worst thing about having no home?

Around the world

Do you enjoy reading books, playing with your toys and going to school? Many children in the world would love to enjoy these things, but they cannot.

Some children have to work more than ten hours a day for very little money.

In some places, children are forced to become slaves. They have to work long hours without a break, and do not go to school. Anti-Slavery International works to stop slavery, and makes sure that all children have the opportunity to go to school, to rest and to play.

What would you miss most if you were forced to work long hours every day?

A charity called ActionAid gets people in Britain to pay a little money each month to help children in poor countries.

CASE STUDY

David Watson is a teacher in Britain. He **sponsors** Alefa (10) in southern Africa through ActionAid. His money has been used to help build a local school for Alefa and her friends living in the village.

♡ War time

Imagine waking up one morning and being told you have to leave your home because a war is going on. This happens to thousands of people every year. Worse still, many children see people being hurt or killed in wars, including their family and friends.

CASE STUDY

This Kurdish family were bombed and forced to leave their home in Iraq. They now live in Britain. The **Refugee** Council helped them to find a home and settle down - very difficult in a country where everyone speaks a different language from you.

In some places, children are taken from their families, forced to become soldiers and fight in wars. Save the Children helps these boys and girls to stop being soldiers and to find their families again.

Save the Children helps child soldiers go back to school.

What would you do if a war forced you to move to a new country?

Raising money

Charities are able to help others, because they are given money. This money is given by **governments**, businesses and people like you and me. Together we give millions of pounds each year.

It can be great fun raising money for charities. It doesn't matter how silly or simple the idea is – as long as it helps. It could be a sponsored walk or bike ride, a sponsored silence or a competition.

Adverts on posters and on TV make things seem attractive so you want to buy them. Charities use adverts to show how children need help.

Charities often get famous people to help draw attention to the problems facing children. England footballer David Seaman and Rugby Union player Paul Volley (pictured here) supported the NSPCC's campaign to stop people being cruel to children.

♥ How you can help

Have you ever helped anyone?
It can feel good to help someone.

You could help by:

● contacting a charity that you are interested in (see pages 30-31) to find out more about what they do. Many charities have children's clubs that include competitions and games, as well as information.

● asking your teacher to get someone from a charity you are interested in to come and talk to your class.

● making sure you are kind to all children you meet, even if they look or behave a bit differently from your other friends. As this book shows, many children have problems but feel and want just the same things as you.

● raising some money for the charity of your choice on your own or through your school. Get your parent or carer or teacher to contact the charity to find out more.

Glossary

abuse — when someone is hurt or forced by another person to do something they do not want to do.

adoption — when a child has new parents and goes to live with them all the time.

disabled — when a person is not able to use a part of their body or to learn in the same way as others.

government — the people who make laws and rule the country.

homeless — when someone doesn't have a home.

polio — a disease that has killed many children and disabled many more, making it difficult for them to use their arms and legs and move around.

refuge — a safe place.

refugee — someone forced to leave their home and find safety in another country.

sponsor — to give someone money to support them.

young person — someone aged between 12 and 18 years.

Contact details

All the charities in this book do many more things to help children than those described. Contact them to find out more.

ActionAid
020 7561 7561
www.actionaid.org

Action Research
01403 210406
www.actionresearch.co.uk

Anti-Slavery International
020 7501 8920
www.antislavery.org

Barnardo's
020 8550 8822
www.barnardos.org.uk

ChildLine
020 7650 3200
www.childline.org.uk
Helpline 0800 1111

Children's Country Holidays Fund
020 7928 6522
www.childrensholidays-
cchf.org

Children's Society
020 7841 4400
www.childrenssociety.org.uk

Centrepoint
020 7426 5300
www.centrepoint.org.uk

Cruse Bereavement Care
www.crusebereavementcare.
org.uk
Helpline 0870 1671677

Great Ormond Street Hospital Children's Charity
020 7916 5678
www.gosh.org

Jubilee Action
01483 894787
www.jubileeaction.co.uk

NCH - Action for Children
020 7704 7000
www.nchafc.org.uk

National Society for the Prevention of
Cruelty to Children (NSPCC)
020 7825 2500
www.nspcc.org.uk
Helpline 0808 800 5000

Refuge
020 7395 7700
Helpline 0870 5995443

The Refugee Council
020 7820 3000
www.refugeecouncil.org.uk

Save the Children
020 7703 5400
www.savethechildren.org.uk

Scope
020 7619 7100
www.scope.org.uk
Helpline 0808 800 3333

UNICEF UK
020 7405 5592
www.unicef.org.uk

Organisations in Australia and New Zealand

Barnardo's Australia
(02) 9281 5510
www.barnardos.org.au

Save the Children Australia
(03) 9811 4999
www.savethechildren.org.au

UNICEF Australia
(02) 9261 2811
www.unicef.com.au

World Vision Australia
(03) 9287 2233
www.worldvision.org.au

Cancer Society of New Zealand
www.cancersoc.org.nz

♥ Index

abuse 16, 18-19, 29
adoption 17, 29
adverts 27

babies 4
bullying 7

death 11
disability 8, 12, 29

families 10, 16-17, 25
famous people 5, 27
feeling better 11, 16, 19
fund-raising 5, 26-27,
    28

helplines 7, 19, 30-31
holidays 15
homeless 20-21, 29
hospital 4, 10
houses 5, 14

illness 4, 8, 10, 13

medicine 8-9
money 5, 14-15, 20, 23,
    26

playing 13, 14, 15

refugees 24, 29

sadness 11
school 6-7, 12, 23, 25
slavery 22

talking 11, 16

war 24-25